# Let a kid be a kid

## (Deja que un niño sea un niño)

# SPIRITUAL FORMATION

CHILDREN ARE AT A CRUCIAL STAGE OF DEVELOPMENT, AND A KIDS' MINISTRY PROVIDES AN ENVIRONMENT WHERE THEY CAN LEARN ABOUT FAITH, VALUES, AND SPIRITUAL PRINCIPLES IN AN AGE-APPROPRIATE MANNER. IT LAYS A STRONG FOUNDATION FOR THEIR SPIRITUAL GROWTH AND RELATIONSHIP WITH GOD.

GTM

# BIBLICAL EDUCATION

A KIDS' MINISTRY INTRODUCES CHILDREN TO THE STORIES, TEACHINGS, AND VALUES OF THE BIBLE. IT HELPS THEM UNDERSTAND THE CORE BELIEFS OF CHRISTIANITY AND FOSTERS A DEEPER UNDERSTANDING OF THEIR FAITH.

# WORSHIP AND PRAYER

CHILDREN CAN PARTICIPATE IN WORSHIP AND PRAYER WITHIN A KIDS' MINISTRY, ALLOWING THEM TO EXPERIENCE AND DEVELOP A PERSONAL CONNECTION WITH GOD. IT HELPS THEM EXPRESS THEIR FEELINGS AND BUILD A PRAYERFUL LIFE.

## COMMUNITY AND FELLOWSHIP:

KIDS' MINISTRY FOSTERS A SENSE OF COMMUNITY AND BELONGING AMONG CHILDREN, WHERE THEY CAN MAKE FRIENDS WHO SHARE SIMILAR BELIEFS AND VALUES. IT CREATES A SUPPORTIVE ENVIRONMENT FOR THEM AND THEIR FAMILIES.

# CHARACTER BUILDING

THROUGH LESSONS, ACTIVITIES, AND INTERACTIONS, KIDS' MINISTRIES INSTILL POSITIVE VALUES SUCH AS KINDNESS, COMPASSION, HONESTY, AND RESPECT.

THESE VALUES CONTRIBUTE TO THE CHARACTER DEVELOPMENT OF CHILDREN AS THEY GROW

# LEADERSHIP AND SERVICE:

KIDS'MINISTRY OFFERS OPPORTUNITIES FOR CHILDREN TO TAKE ON LEADERSHIP ROLES AND ENGAGE IN SERVICE PROJECTS, TEACHING THEM THE IMPORTANCE OF GIVING BACK AND BEING ACTIVELY INVOLVED IN THEIR COMMUNITY

# FAMILY ENGAGEMENT

A WELL-STRUCTURED KIDS' MINISTRY INVOLVES PARENTS AND GUARDIANS, ENCOURAGING THEM TO PARTICIPATE IN THEIR CHILDREN'S SPIRITUAL JOURNEY. IT STRENGTHENS FAMILY BONDS.

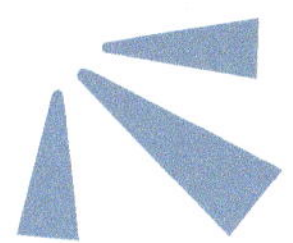

# FUTURE CHURCH GROWTH

CHILDREN ARE THE FUTURE OF THE CHURCH. BY INVESTING IN THEIR SPIRITUAL GROWTH AND DEVELOPMENT, A CHURCH ENSURES A STRONG FOUNDATION FOR ITS FUTURE GROWTH AND SUSTAINABILITY.

# INCLUSIVITY

KIDS' MINISTRY WELCOMES CHILDREN FROM ALL BACKGROUNDS AND ABILITIES, CREATING AN INCLUSIVE AND DIVERSE ENVIRONMENT THAT EMBRACES EVERYONE WITH LOVE AND ACCEPTANCE.

# JOYFUL LEARNING: A

KIDS' MINISTRY OFTEN INCORPORATES FUN AND ENGAGING ACTIVITIES, MAKING LEARNING ABOUT FAITH AN ENJOYABLE EXPERIENCE FOR CHILDREN. THIS APPROACH HELPS CREATE A POSITIVE ASSOCIATION WITH CHURCH AND RELIGIOUS PRACTICES.

MINISTRY AT CHURCH IS CRUCIAL FOR NURTURING THE SPIRITUAL GROWTH OF CHILDREN, PROVIDING THEM WITH A SOLID UNDERSTANDING OF FAITH, AND FOSTERING A SENSE OF COMMUNITY AND BELONGING. IT PLAYS A SIGNIFICANT ROLE IN SHAPING THE FUTURE OF BOTH THE CHILDREN AND THE CHURCH AS A WHOLE.

IT PLAYS A SIGNIFICANT ROLE IN SHAPING THE FUTURE OF BOTH THE CHILDREN AND THE CHURCH AS A WHOLE.

"TO MY WONDERFUL KIDS, I'M SORRY IT TOOK ME SO LONG TO TRULY HEAR FROM GOD. PLEASE FORGIVE ME FOR NOT TEACHING YOU HIS WAYS WHEN YOU WERE CHILDREN."

www.ingramcontent.com/pod-product-compliance
Lightning Source LLC
Chambersburg PA
CBHW042126110726
48006CB00003B/778
* 9 7 9 8 8 6 9 0 9 4 9 1 9 *